Self-published using lulu.com online services.

Revised edition

All artwork and images created and/or provided by the author unless otherwise noted.

ISBN 978-1-716-25177-1

ty nxt

thank you, next

a collection of poems
by James Stevens

thank you to the shark, the bear and the pup
for motivation, support and inspiration

I am nothing if not honest, I find it difficult to lie - and to that, I admit that poetry does not come easy.

My poetry is a conduit for my emotions to speak freely.

I struggle to hide meanings in metaphors and revelations in rhyme. Poetry is therapy, when the words refuse to turn to sound; I let my heart speak or scream through my fingers. Poetry is subjective; there are rules to be followed, that is for sure, but these rules **can be bent.**

A sentence is a poem if it moves you.

Table of Contents

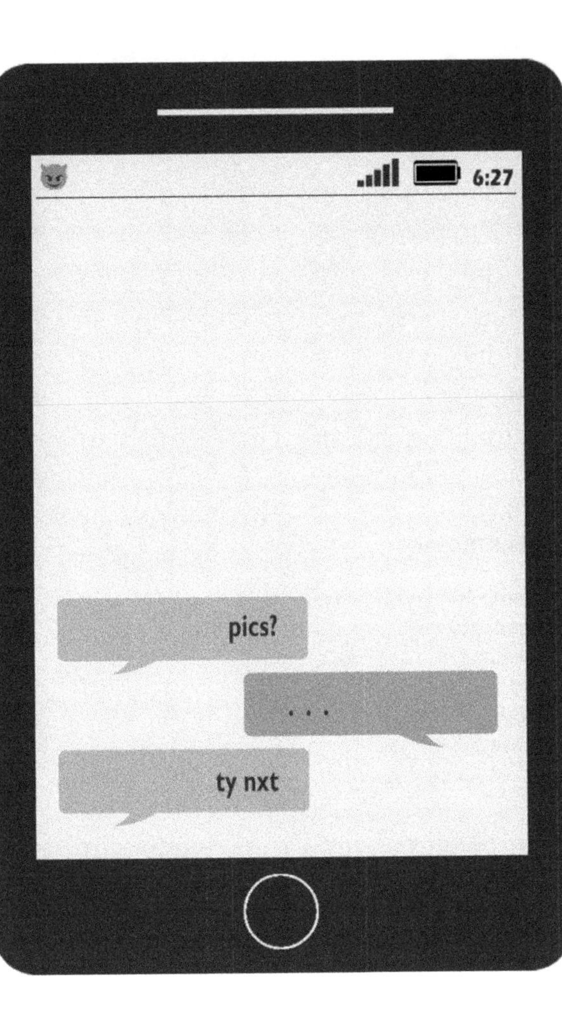
6:27
pics?
. . .
ty nxt

HEARTBREAK I

heart
beating
bleeding
red
stop
brake

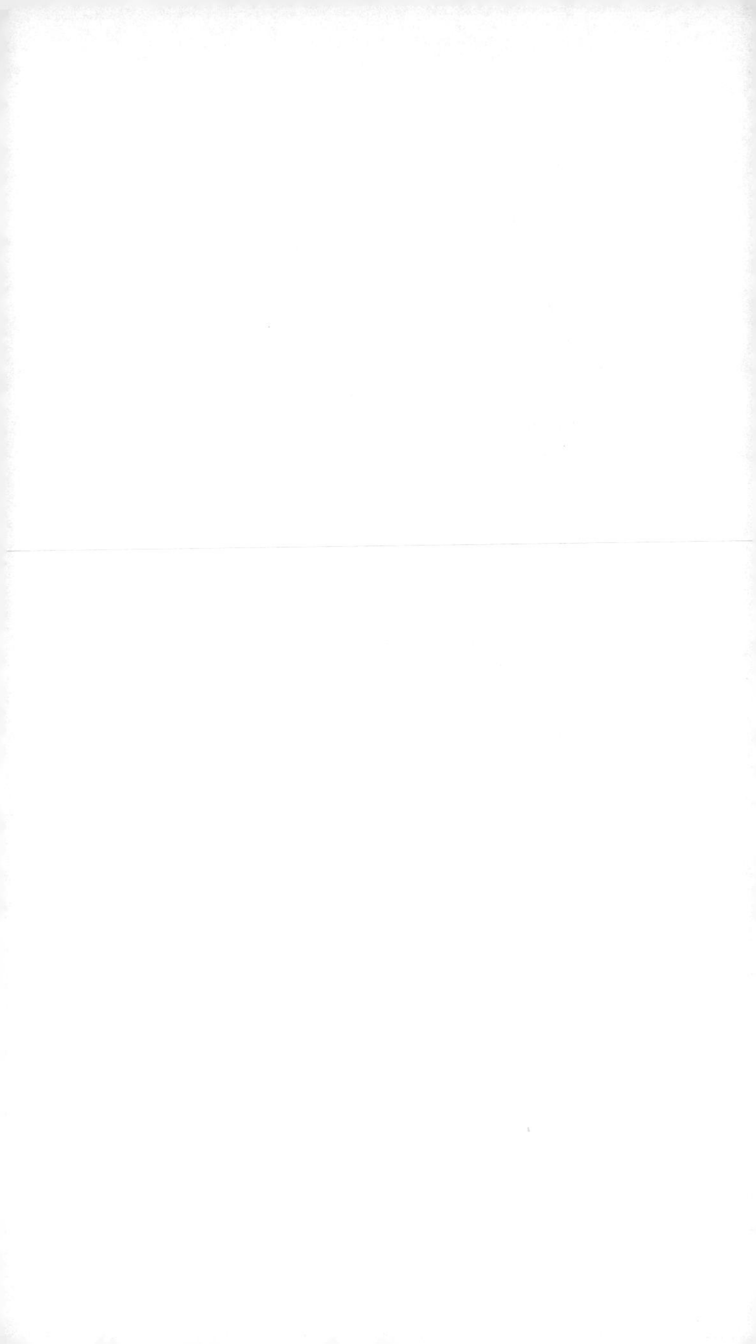

the buzz

the thoughts buzz inside your head
so loud to you, yet silent reverberating
through your skull,
buzzing fills your eyes, your vision dims from the
outside in
suddenly laser focused on the globe within your head
in your head, in your head you can see it all
details: every pinching thought
stacked
    on top
        of
  one
    another
the buzzing flows down the spine, muscles tense
sensing danger, fear.
the body rigid unsure how to respond
buzz to a vibration to a pulse
chest tightens, breathing erratic

PANIC

TOO much, TOO quick
inhale-exhale inhale-exhale
compensate, slow down, just breathe
the humming throws you off
...inhale...
holdyourbreath

three, two, one

e x h a l e

and the cycle repeats, and the cycle repeats, and the cycle repeats, and the cycle repeats, and the cycle repeats, and the cycle repeats, and the cycle repeats...

i freeze

cold and silent
reaching into the haze
of a past
finding the familiar
touch still cold
so cold
as I melt
letting go
passing by
not looking back
looking back
still so hazy
caught a chill
moving slowly
slower still
until…
until..
until.

vending machine of love

Four quarters: a dollar now you've got a new toy,
handsome and smart your playful new boy,
to take out on dates, while I missed my chance
all that he wants is to get into your pants

Or rather you out of them, ain't that the way
on Grindr and Scruff, the apps for the gay
sixty bare chests, thick thighs and more
waiting for you to dive in and explore

The way that you feel it really don't matter
'cuz here on the app you're just meat on the platter
they tear off the pieces that they want the most
each man-feast beginning with 'hey, do you host?'

Still each night ends like the last night before
you sleep all alone, but feel like a whore.

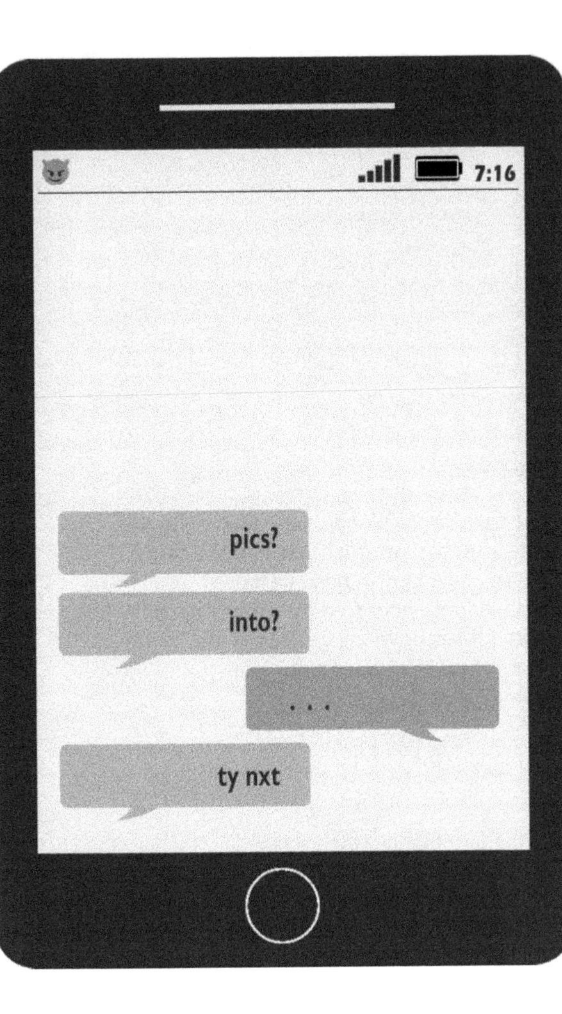
7:16
pics?
into?
. . .
ty nxt

LUST

the town drunk wanders the rows of houses
late after the last drink well into the dark
his key held tight in hand he moves
from door to door free hand fumbling at the knockers
with his key hovering before the lock he smiles
but none will let the drunk
come inside

clouds for my coffee

I walk into the room – look at me
I want eyes to follow me
I need eyes to follow me
watching what I do, where I go
who I talk to and who I snub
I need them to want to be near me
I want to look over my shoulder to see them look
away
afraid, ashamed of their desire for me
they love to watch
I love when they watch
they all want to know what it's like
to know my touch, taste my lips, feel my breath and
know my caress
and I... I want them to want it
they'll want it
and want it
and I'll never give in
to be seen – by all of them
to be wanted – by all of them
it's what I need
if they don't
who am I?

shadow of the grid

wake up in the box top left looking out	neighbours come and go depending	on the mood the tribes converge
and when he comes... you		and the animals come to feed
the fleeting feeling fills you up	just the right amount of pain left	flesh back between teeth

night's touch

First, in a way. The last was fourteen ago
Understand that it means far more
Choice, yes – always that, never forced
Keeping like champagne – for a special occasion
Given but only to one with heart
Regretful of some, envious of others
If not for this... what else have I to offer you
Nothing new, nothing special or all that unique
Determined not to falter, I try to
Resist, but damn if not for that sweet song.

the GRID

I am no face in the grid
I don’t fit with them
I am not ripped, nor rich, nor a scholar
I am not one of the anonymous

You won’t find my torso tangled in the web
no perfect chiselled six-pack, or perky perfect nipples,
no shots of chest hair trimmed just right
you won’t find me in my underwear,
pictured in poses that only beg you to enter

I don’t belong to this crowd
I loathe, desire,
envy and admire them
crave fleeting moments with them
but I am not them
I do not fit in their grid

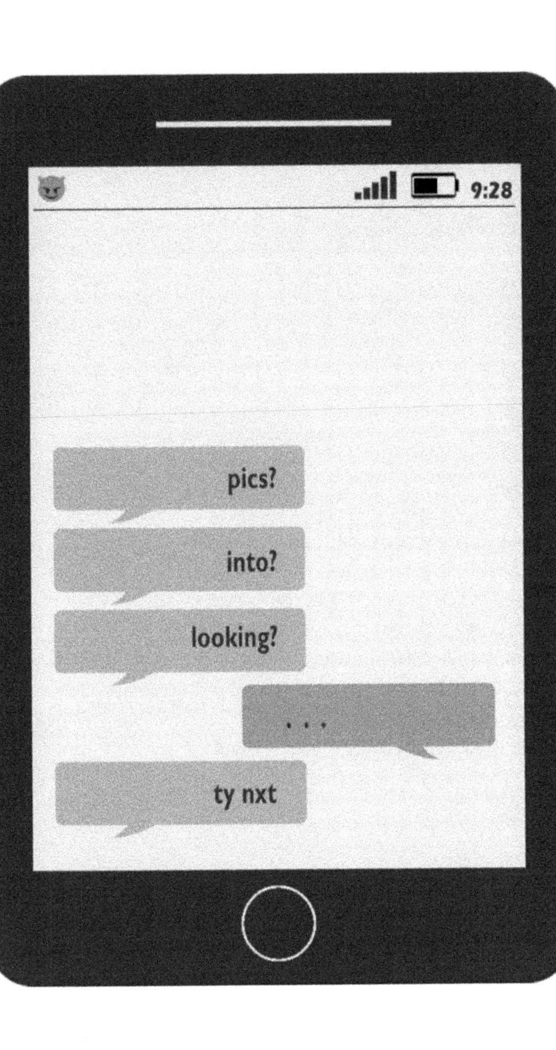
9:28
pics?
into?
looking?
. . .
ty nxt

LOVE

Love is the storm that you so
foolishly live to chase.
Always out of reach you run only to find
the wet each cloud leaves behind.
Stand still, stop chasing and the storm will come to you
but the rain won't quench the thirst or desire
so you run and you chase
the next storm out on the horizon

12:01am

Utopian observations delusional at best
Often relying on the fears of ignorant sheep to
Yield the tastiest of meat for the grindr.
Envious of the night calls and
Killing for a cascade of 'little deaths'
I long for the touch of your lip to my
Lips and your hips to my hip as we slip
Into toxic waves of deliciously naughty choices
Never to breach the surface for
Air, stealing breaths from one another, each
Exhale pulling us closer to the dark end
Soon to be nothing but dust at midnight.

a can of sweet corn

While on bended knee,
I'll ask this of you
Please with this ring
take my heart and be true
to a love that we've built
despite hardship and time
to be with you, you know
that I'd melt my last dime
and if no be the answer
to me you must give
I shall fall by this sword
for I'll have no life to live
as nothing on earth
compares quite to you
these words may be corny
but with love... know they're true

the end of june

we met in front of thirty-one
walking East to watch the sun
set over a hill at the park
holding hands we go in the dark
and at my front door we kiss
sir, it's that feeling I miss
of your arms wrapped 'round my chest
I'd forgotten all of the rest
next from work I walk you home
night after that was one spent alone
twenty-four later watching movies we laugh
soon though we find we are only on half
of the couch while you move close to cuddle
ugh – my heart is becoming a puddle
but you tell me that you felt the same
seems as though cupid has taken his aim

cling wrap

holding tight
never too much
taught
but removable
what's under – accessible
preserved
saved for later
tomorrow
a midnight snack
another taste
then put it back
stretch the wrap
no need to tear
no need
but even gentle hands
fumble

poison app(le)

some of us, not all of us
find it easy to emote
because of this, the some of us
will either sink or float
some will exceed at laughter
or songs that make you cry
while others will be silent
staring blankly at the sky
a lonely life is not the way
to act so independent
you'll see that with him by your side
each experience -- transcendent
he's half of you, you're half of him
yet still two separate people
different, oh so different yet
they treat each as an equal
but secrets and lies beneath the surface
will always disturb the calm
and the poison that you love so much
you hold it in your palm

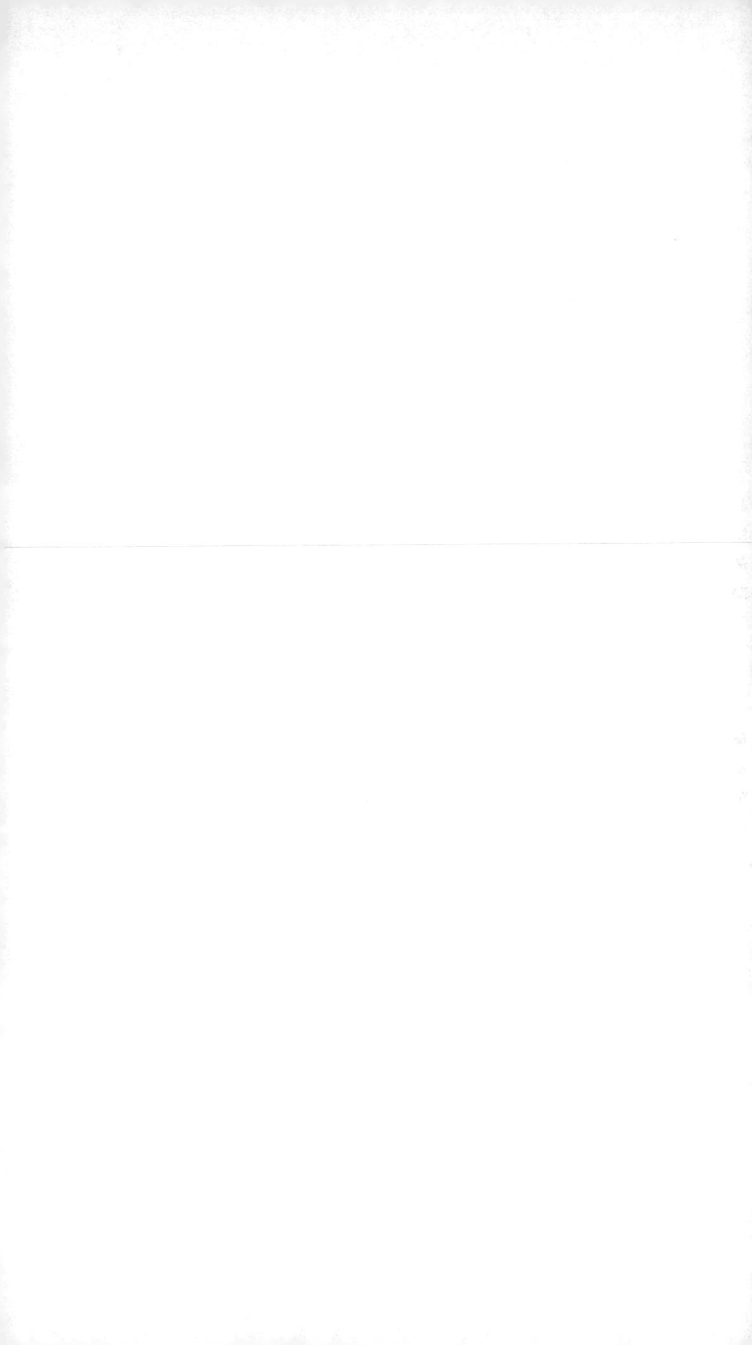

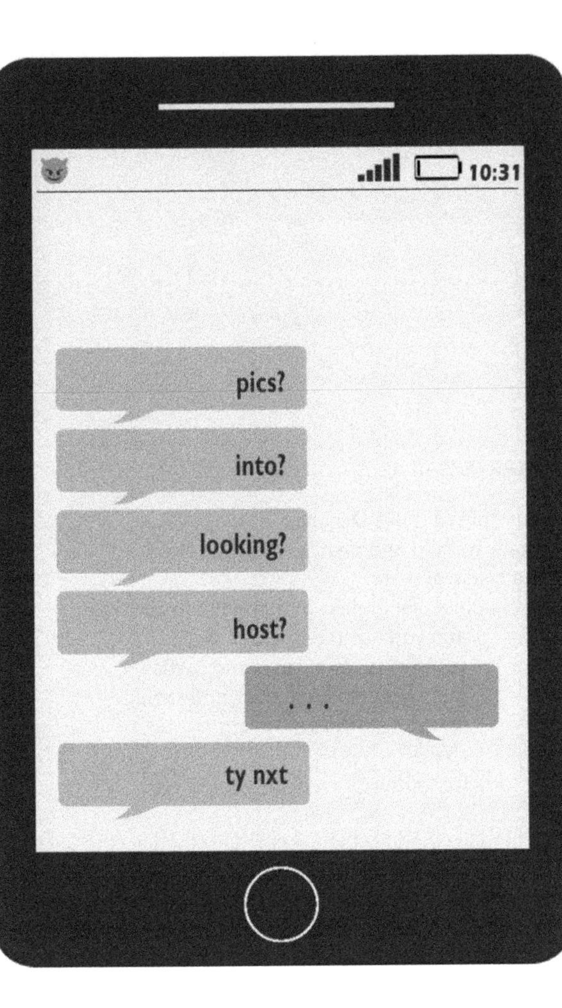
10:31
pics?
into?
looking?
host?
. . .
ty nxt

HEARTBREAK II

Heartbreak is like the brick
heavy to hold and deadly when struck
the cause of pain,
rivers flow over cheeks into puddles in your lap
    and you use the bricks to build
    your walls, your cages and castles
    build them tall and thick and strong
    forget not ever
    space
    for a door

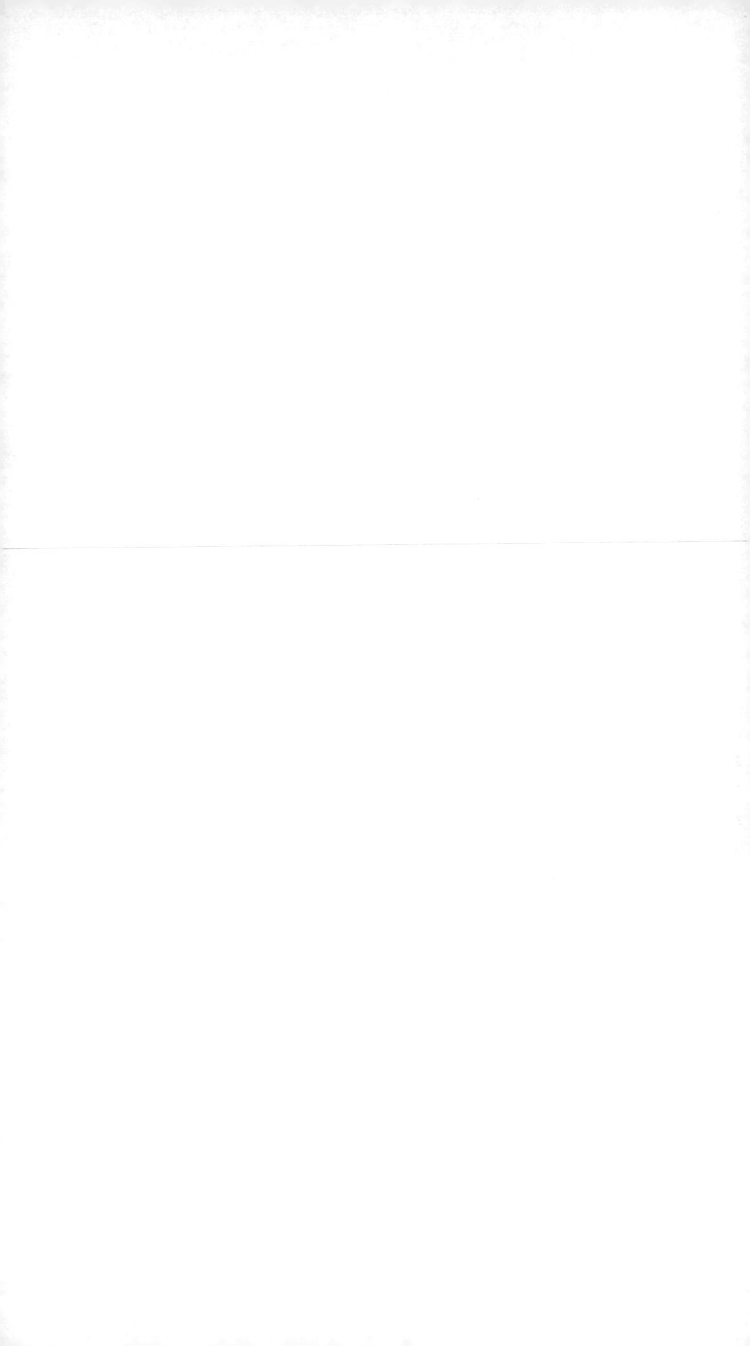

the menu

you place your order
set the option list aside
clink glasses (cheers!)
we laugh – you look
to the menu
browsing meals
just a quick glance
the food comes
what you've ordered
what you've asked for
what you said you wanted most
still you don't relinquish
the menu
as you eat
you look – finger sliding down
the page of choice
so many choices
right in front of you
and you eat
eat and look
planning that next meal
to fill the next hunger
before you even feel it

clusterfuck of emotion

click-click-click-click-click,
faster and faster still as tiny hammers pound
on plastic tablets etched with the alphanumeric code
each click, each tap
a letter, then a word,
forming sentence after sentence of our demise

fires burn in the rusted furnace of my heart
cracked, the heat escapes, and the flames spread
the fire eats at my foundation and I crumble within

swaying in the open window breeze hangs a cage
inside there is no singing bird,
no monster or creature of wonder
just a handful of glittering dust and a key

the smoke clears
and all that stands in the charred remains
is the cage, its contents and me

A minute, an hour a day goes by
a week, a fortnight, a month and more
painstaking work rebuilding glass hearts
my fingers drip with red determination

at last, only one piece is all that remains
the final piece to complete my fragile glass
is your gentle hand to turn the key

don't wake me

you had so many others
in your hand
                                        waiting

so many options
                                        wanting

while I slept
while I dreamt
when I left

the addiction
knock-knocks
you answer

if I check
would I find
and I did
every time

hard to trust
to believe

while I sleep
while I dream

was it easy for you to let go

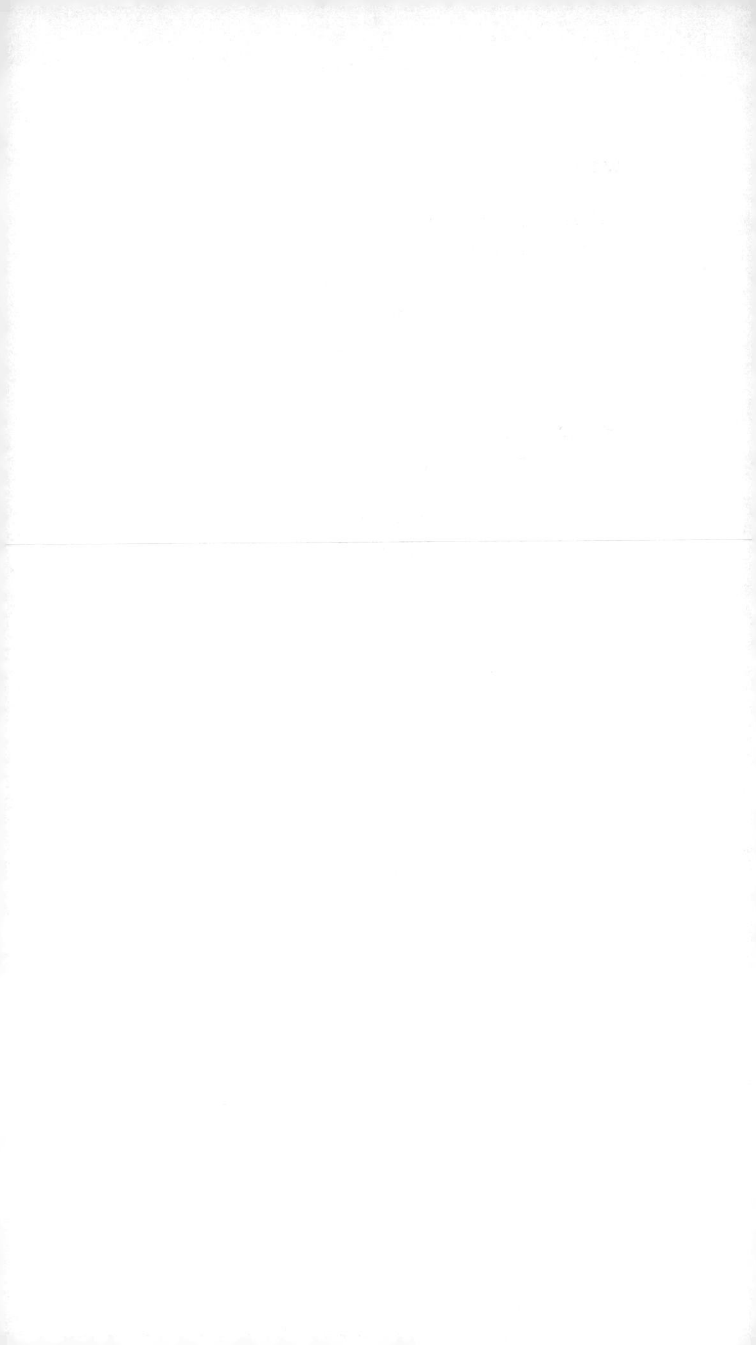

we all

I know that I made promises --
said I'd always lend a hand
but when you showed up crying
I found I couldn't be your friend

my headphones in, the music loud...
I had to tune you out
I couldn't hear, but I could see
the tears and how you'd shout

I had to turn my back to you
(out of sight and out of mind)
I promise dear it's good for you...
I'm trying to be kind

time passes and I tell myself
you've no more tears to shed
I turn and swear I looked for you...
but found empty space instead

to be honest I didn't search for long;
I figured you were fine
I'd seen you go through moods like this
all the god damn time

so when I went to bed that night,
I thought of it nothing much
it did feel weird when two days later
you still hadn't been in touch

I sent a text and checked online
but couldn't find you green
I asked around to figure out
when last you had been seen

But no one seemed to know
just where you may have went
then late that night I got an email
that you had schedule-sent

It told me that you loved me
and just how hard you'd tried
but despite the smiles and laughter
you still felt sad inside

you felt like you were a burden...
just a pain to be around
my brain begins to comprehend,
my heart -- it starts to pound

I know by now just what you've done
and that I am already too late
I cry and wish and even beg
to turn back the hands of fate

But what you've done is permanent.
No chance to take it back
and many lives are shattered now,
self-blame we all unpack

I wish that I had been there for you;
the night you came and cried
but, I my dear had pain then too
that I tried to keep inside

I didn't want to burden you
with all my stupid thoughts
but now I sit here lonely
as my stomach turns in knots

11:02
hey
ty nxt

HOPE

to see the future of love
do not use your eyes,
open instead your heart to me
and there the truth will rise

little steps

I move on
I keep going
I look back
slightly slowing
to see you there
frowns both growing
it isn't fair
emotions showing
wipe the tear
both of us knowing
each heart still beats
and ever glowing
for the other
on eggshells tiptoeing
we sleep through it
dreams overflowing

prioritize you

and truth be told
that's where it is
deep within your heart
love doesn't come from any other
if you have yet to start
to love yourself it does sound easy
and words they often are
but that worth doing is hard and rough
and sure to leave a scar
but do not let that stop you
from hunting the joy you seek
it's when you least expect it you see
that love will often peek

twenty7

still just playing make believe
wishing on broken stars
fantasies and fairy tales
leaving unseen scars

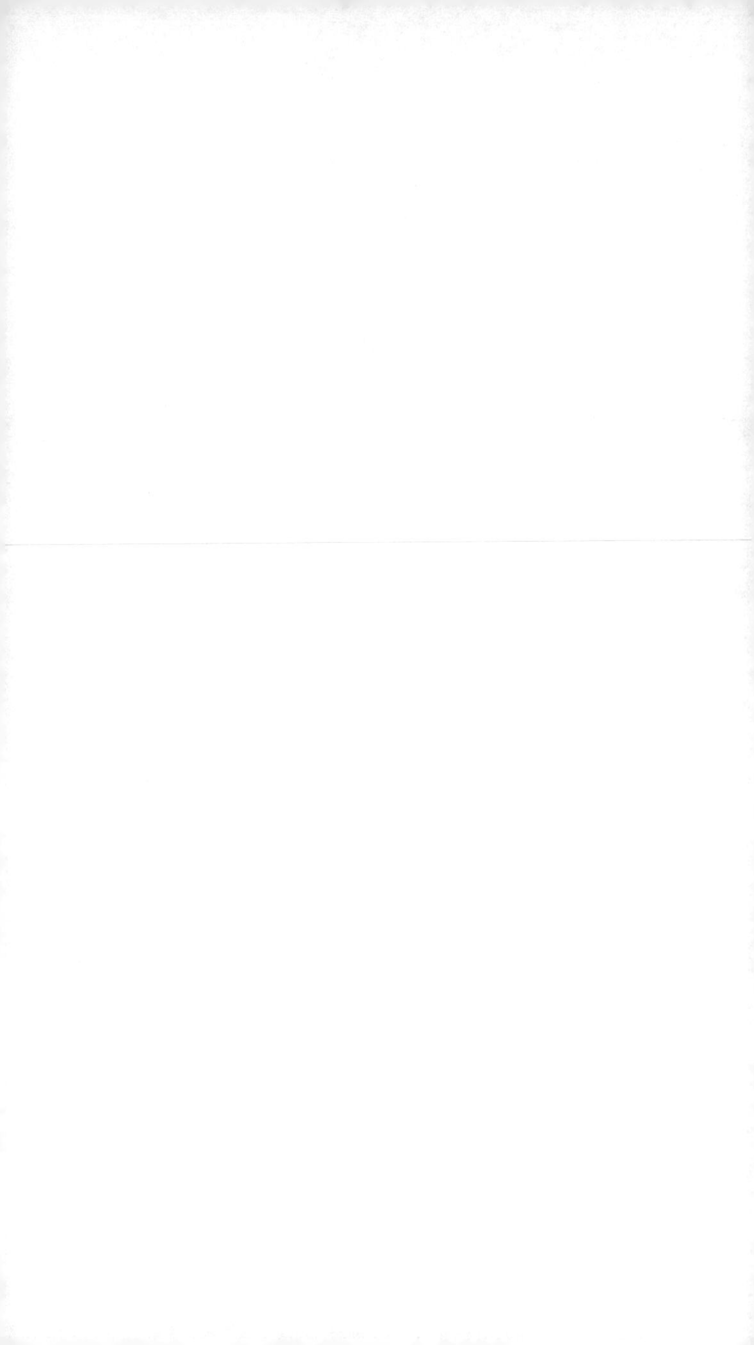

11:11

hey

hi... how are you?

www.ingramcontent.com/pod-product-compliance
Ingram Content Group UK Ltd.
Pitfield, Milton Keynes, MK11 3LW, UK
UKHW020414250726
13967UKWH00007B/2641

9 781716 251771